---

*God is with you. He will not
fail you or forsake you.*

1 CHRONICLES 28:20

From:

1

⌂ ZondervanPublishingHouse
Mail Drop B20
Grand Rapids, Michigan 49530
http://www.zondervan.com

Senior Editor: Gwen Ellis
Project Editor: Pat Matuszak
Art Director: Brian Scharp
Designer: Gayle Raymer Design
Illustrations: Erika Lebarre
Printed in China
00 01 02/HK/5 4 3

Footprints

by Margaret Fishback Powers

Footprints

One night I dreamed a dream.
I was walking along the beach with my Lord.
Across the dark sky flashed scenes from my life.
For each scene, I noticed two sets
of footprints in the sand,
one belonging to me and one to my Lord.
When the last scene of my life shot before me
I looked back at the footprints in the sand.
There was only one set of footprints.
I realized that this was at the lowest
and saddest times of my life.
This always bothered me
and I questioned the Lord
about my dilemma.

"Lord, you told me when I decided to follow You,
You would walk and talk with me all the way.
But I'm aware that during the most troublesome
times of my life
there is only one set of footprints.
I just don't understand why,
when I needed You most,
You leave me."
He whispered, "My precious child,
I love you and will never leave you
never, ever, during your trials and testings.
When you saw only one set of footprints
it was then that I carried you."

$\mathcal{D}$on't ignore your dreams.
God can use our dreams to tell us
something about his character or
to assure us of his promises.

*O*n my bed I remember you;
I think of you through the watches
of the night.

$\mathcal{D}$reams that are inspired
by the Holy Spirit are worth
retelling and following.

I will pour out my Spirit
   on all people.
Your sons and daughters
   will prophesy,
your old men will dream dreams,
your young men will see visions.

JOEL 2:28

*W*hen God speaks to us such as in a dream, he will help us understand it. He will reassure us of his presence with us and help make those dreams come true.

"When a prophet of the LORD is among you, I reveal myself to him in visions, I speak to him in dreams."

NUMBERS 12:6

Just as a consistent program of walking improves muscle tone and strengthens the heart, so our spiritual life will also reap benefits when we are consistent in walking with the Lord.

12

I will walk among you
and be your God, and you
will be my people.

LEVITICUS 26:12

13

For there's no other way
To be happy in Jesus
But to trust and obey.

JOHN H. SAMMIS

Jesus said: "Whoever does the will of my Father in heaven is my brother and sister and mother."

MATTHEW 12:50

God wants our walk with him to
be a joyful, shared togetherness.
Such an intimate walk of faith with
the Lord will assure us of his love.

*M*oses said to the LORD,
"If your Presence does not go
with us, do not send us up
from here."

EXODUS 33:15

O Joy that seekest me
   through pain,
I cannot close my heart to Thee;
I trace the rainbow through
   the rain,
And feel the promise is not vain
That morn shall tearless be.

GEORGE MATHESON

If we walk in the light, as he is in the light, we have fellowship with one another, and the blood of Jesus, his Son, purifies us from all sin.

1 JOHN 1:7

As we face the uncertainties that today may bring, we have the assurance that God knows what we are facing. He is in touch with what is happening to us, and he is concerned.

Surely God is my salvation;
I will trust and not be afraid.
The LORD, the LORD, is my
strength and my song;
he has become my salvation.

ISAIAH 12:2

God is the God of grace and
hope. With God's perspective, we
can trace his hand on our lives and
see that he has transformed the
bad things to good, just as he
promised he would.

*T*hose who hope in the LORD
   will renew their strength.
They will soar on wings like
   eagles;
they will run and not grow weary,
   they will walk and not be faint.

ISAIAH 40:31

23

For each scene, I noticed two sets
of footprints in the sand,
one belonging to me and one
to my Lord.

He will teach us his ways,
so that we may walk in his paths.

ISAIAH 2:3

We all go through times when
life seems to overwhelm us.
The Bible reassures us that God's
presence is with us to help us,
even when we don't realize it.

Jesus said, "Do not let your hearts be troubled. Trust in God; trust also in me."

JOHN 14:1

I've found a Friend, O such a Friend!
   So kind and true and tender,
So wise a Counselor and Guide,
   So mighty a Defender!
From Him who loves me now so well,
   What pow'r my soul can sever?
Shall life or death or earth or hell?
   No – I am His forever.

JAMES G. SMALL

*You are my hiding place;
you will protect me from trouble
and surround me with songs
of deliverance.*

PSALM 32:7

There is hope for all of us.
There is light. Jesus Christ,
the Son of God is our hope and
light in darkness.

You are my lamp, O LORD;
the LORD turns my darkness
into light.

2 SAMUEL 22:29

Our faith can be strengthened if
we will wait patiently and trust
God's heart's desire to make us
more like himself.

*O*ur light and momentary troubles are achieving for us an eternal glory that far outweighs them all. So we fix our eyes not on what is seen, but on what is unseen. For what is seen is temporary, but what is unseen is eternal.

2 CORINTHIANS 4:17-18

The Lord is ...our friend. He enjoys walking with us as our companion on life's pathway. And he brings blessing into our lives when we walk closely with him.

*B*e joyful in hope,
patient in affliction,
faithful in prayer.

ROMANS 12:12

The awareness of God's presence with us is encouraging and heart-warming. It is as if we were two friends seated beside a rippling brook, enjoying a gentle breeze on a warm spring afternoon.

"Here I am! I stand at the door and knock. If anyone hears my voice and opens the door, I will come in and eat with him, and he with me," says the Lord.

REVELATION 3:20

37

On our journey home,
our close fellowship with the Lord
will help us cross the rough places
without the slightest care.

*A*sk where the good way is,
and walk in it, and you will find
rest for your souls.

JEREMIAH 6:16

*W*hen we have experienced God's forgiveness, we are new creatures. We do not need to live a life of regrets, but rather we can live with a forward-looking hope of glory!

*Therefore, if anyone is in Christ,
he is a new creation; the old has
gone, the new has come!*

2 CORINTHIANS 5:17

God never changes. He is the God of grace. He is the God of hope. He is the God of love, who offers us a life free of regrets.

*C*ome ... *let us walk*
in the light of the LORD.

ISAIAH 2:5

Whenever we do look back
over our lives we must do so
with God's perspective, without
remorse or regrets and live in
God's peace and joy.

*A*nd we know that in all things
God works for the good of those
who love him, who have been
called according to his purpose.

ROMANS 8:28

To my surprise, I noticed that
many times along the path
of my life there was only one
set of footprints...
But I've learned that God is
always with us, in our joy and in
our pain, in the good times
and in the bad times.

God has said,
"Never will I leave you;
never will I forsake you."

HEBREWS 13:5

*H*is steadfast love and faithfulness are promises we can cling to; promises to bring us joy when we face loneliness.

*A*nd Jesus told his disciples,
"And surely I am with you always,
to the very end of the age."

MATTHEW 28:20

*W*hen loneliness overtakes us,
we need to remember that we are
not alone. God has promised to be
with us. Lean on his promises
and receive his peace.

*B*e strong and courageous.
Do not be afraid or terrified ...
for the LORD your God goes with
you; he will never leave you
nor forsake you.

DEUTERONOMY 31:6

Though we may face trouble,
difficulties, sadness and pain,
God is still in control, and he
is always with us.

My flesh and my heart may
fail, but God is the strength of my
heart and my portion forever.

PSALM 73:26

We must remember to listen closely to God's voice when trouble rages around us. When the agonies of life begin to crush us, God has not moved away from us.

"*When* you pass through the waters, I will be with you; and when you pass through the rivers, they will not sweep over you. ..." says the LORD.

ISAIAH 43:2

No sorrow is so deep
that God cannot feel it with us.
And God wants to help deliver us
from it. He wants to bring us his
divine comfort.

This I call to mind and therefore I have hope: Because of the LORD's great love we are not consumed, for his compassions never fail. They are new every morning; great is your faithfulness.

LAMENTATIONS 3:21-23

*N*o situation is ever
without God's presence.

"Do not fear, for I am
with you; do not be dismayed,
for I am your God. I will
strengthen you and help you;
I will uphold you with my
righteous right hand."

ISAIAH 41:10

God sees tomorrow more clearly than we see yesterday. We don't need to fret! The future is completely in his hands!

*W*hen they heard that the
LORD was concerned about them
and had seen their misery, they
bowed down and worshiped.

EXODUS 4:31

61

Neither the sun, nor the Son, has gone out of business. He is with us. A new day will dawn and the Lord will bring himself to the center of our problems.

*L*et us then approach the throne
of grace with confidence,
so that we may receive mercy
and find grace to help us in
our time of need.

HEBREWS 4:16

Prayer is the only way to cut those knots of worry and care and grant us God's peace instead.

*T*he LORD is with you when
you are with him. If you seek him,
he will be found by you.

2 CHRONICLES 15:2

*A*nd I questioned the Lord
about my dilemma...

When we face questions,
we need to get our arms around
God's wisdom.

If any of you lacks wisdom, he should ask God, who gives generously to all without finding fault, and it will be given to him.

JAMES 1:5

God doesn't mind our questions
when we come to him with
a seeking heart.

I will instruct you and teach you in the way you should go; I will counsel you and watch over you," says the LORD.

PSALM 32:8

God is bigger than any question
we can ask. And he often will give
us the answers we seek
in his Word.

*T*rust in the LORD with
all your heart and lean not on
your own understanding; in all
your ways acknowledge him,
and he will make your
paths straight.

PROVERBS 3:5-6

When we find ourselves questioning God's reason for allowing certain things to happen, we must stop, remember God's faithfulness and depend upon his grace.

Let us acknowledge the LORD; let us press on to acknowledge him. As surely as the sun rises, he will appear; he will come to us like the winter rains, like the spring rains that water the earth.

HOSEA 6:3

God has a plan for us. He cares about our dilemmas, hears our heartfelt cries and will answer us in ways that will astonish us and fill our hearts with songs of joy.

"For I know the plans I have for you," declares the LORD, "plans to prosper you and not to harm you, plans to give you hope and a future."

JEREMIAH 29:11

God can help us with the difficult, life-changing decisions.

The LORD says, "I guide you in the way of wisdom and lead you along straight paths."

PROVERBS 4:11

When we decide to follow the Lord, it means we must live our lives the way he wants us to, following his commands and yielding to his control.

Forgetting what is behind and straining toward what is ahead, I press on toward the goal to win the prize for which God has called me heavenward in Christ Jesus.

PHILIPPIANS 3:13-14

"Lord, you told me when I
decided to follow You,
You would walk and talk with me
all the way."

*T*he LORD will guide you
always; he will satisfy your needs
in a sun-scorched land and will
strengthen your frame. You will be
like a well-watered garden, like a
spring whose waters never fail.

ISAIAH 58:11

$\mathcal{G}$od's Word becomes our
road map for our daily walk
with the Savior.

Your word is a lamp to my feet
and a light for my path,
O LORD.

PSALM 119:105

*H*is Word reminds us
of his power, his provision
and his sovereignty.

*C*ommit to the LORD
whatever you do, and your
plans will succeed.

PROVERBS 16:3

Be Thou my Vision, O Lord
of my heart,
Nought be all else to me,
save that Thou art;
Thou my best thought, by day or
by night,
Waking or sleeping, Thy presence
my light.

TRADITIONAL, TRANSLATION BY
MARY E. BYRNE

I will praise the LORD
who counsels me;
even at night my heart
instructs me.

PSALM 16:7

$H$is Word reminds us
of his love.

This I call to mind and therefore I have hope: Because of the LORD's great love we are not consumed, for his compassions never fail. They are new every morning; great is your faithfulness.

LAMENTATIONS 3:21-23

Let's enjoy the time with God as
he walks and talks with us each
day, wherever we are, for "this God
is our God for ever and ever; he
will be our guide even to the end"

(PSALM 48:14).

90

The LORD will fulfill for me; your love, O LORD, endures forever.

PSALM 138:8

$\mathcal{D}$uring the most troublesome
times of my life there is only one
set of footprints...

*W*hy are you downcast, O my
soul? Why so disturbed within
me? Put your hope in God,
for I will yet praise him, my
Savior and my God.

PSALM 43:5-6

We are fearful of the unknown.
But God's Word reminds us to
trust, to believe, to hope.

You have been my hope, O Sovereign LORD, *my confidence since my youth.*

PSALM 71:5

God will never let us down.
He promises us his strength,
his peace, his comfort and his presence. All we need to do is depend
on him. We can never break
God's promises by leaning
on them.

*T*he eternal God is your refuge,
and underneath are the
everlasting arms.

DEUTERONOMY 33:27

Those things we consider difficulties are often God's opportunities for our greater blessing.

"Call upon me in the day of trouble; I will deliver you, and you will honor me," says the LORD.

PSALM 50:15

*H*ave you ever wondered, "Why
did this have to happen?"
God can help us with those
"Why?" questions.

*W*hen times are good, be happy; but when times are bad, consider: God has made the one as well as the other.

ECCLESIASTES 7:14

When faced with bewildering circumstances we are tempted to ask "Why?" But a better question to ask is "What do you have in mind now, Lord?"

Call to me and I will answer you and tell you great and unsearchable things you do not know," says the LORD.

JEREMIAH 33:3

$\mathcal{P}$ut away all doubts. Cast out all confusion. Stand firm in the work of the Lord and find a renewed faith following in his footsteps.

$\mathcal{J}$esus said, "Blessed are you
who hunger now, for you will be
satisfied. Blessed are you who
weep now, for you will laugh."

LUKE 6:21

He whispered,
"My precious child..."

As God's children, our Father
knows us by name.

How ow great is the love the
Father has lavished on us, that we
should be called children of God!

1 JOHN 3:1

As children of God we can trust that our Father will provide for us.

Jesus said, "Your Father knows what you need before you ask him."

MATTHEW 6:8

*O*ur loving Father cares for us
as a shepherd cares for his sheep.

*The sheep listen to his voice.
He calls his own sheep by name
and leads them out. When he
has brought out all his own, he
goes on ahead of them, and his
sheep follow him because they
know his voice.*

JOHN 10:3-4

"*I* love you and will never leave
you never, ever, during your trials
and testings."

When God promises never
to leave us, he means just
what he says.

"Though the mountains be shaken and the hills be removed, yet my unfailing love for you will not be shaken nor my covenant of peace be removed," says the LORD, who has compassion on you.

ISAIAH 54:10

God's encouragement breathes new possibilities into impossible circumstances. And he will work his will in every circumstance.

Jesus said, "Look at the birds of the air; they do not sow or reap or store away in barns, and yet your heavenly Father feeds them. Are you not much more valuable than they? Who of you by worrying can add a single hour to his life?"

MATTHEW 6:26-27

*"W*hen you saw only one set
of footprints it was then
that I carried you."

"*My* grace is sufficient for you, for my power is made perfect in weakness," says the LORD.

2 CORINTHIANS 12:9

Since God is our strong
Provider, we can be assured
that he is in control of every
aspect of our lives.

*B*efore they call I will answer;
while they are still speaking I will
hear," says the LORD.

ISAIAH 65:24

The Lord will prepare
the way before us.
He will never leave us.

No eye has seen, no ear has heard, no mind has conceived what God has prepared for those who love him.

1 CORINTHIANS 2:9

*O*ur God is strong enough to carry us, but also gentle enough to enfold us in his loving embrace.

The LORD longs to be gracious to you; he rises to show you compassion. For the LORD is a God of justice. Blessed are all who wait for him!

ISAIAH 30:18

*A*s our strong Provider carries us over the rough places in our lives, he speaks words of peace and blessing to our wounded hearts.

The LORD makes me lie down in green pastures, he leads me beside quiet waters, he restores my soul. He guides me in paths of righteousness for his name's sake.

PSALM 23:2-3

The Creator of the universe
calls me his child and his friend.
What a blessing! What a privilege!

*T*aste and see
that the LORD is good.

PSALM 34:8

God's presence with us is no
pipe-dream. It is a reality.
It is a dream come true.

Jesus left his disciples with a great
promise that is still true for us today:
Jesus said, "Surely I am with you
always, to the very end of the age."

MATTHEW 28:20